50 Low-Calorie Dessert Recipes for Home

By: Kelly Johnson

Table of Contents

- Greek Yogurt with Honey and Berries
- Baked Apples with Cinnamon
- Chia Seed Pudding
- Banana Ice Cream
- Berry Sorbet
- Mango Coconut Popsicles
- Fruit Salad with Mint
- Light Lemon Bars
- Apple Nachos
- Watermelon Slush
- Baked Pears with Almonds
- Low-Calorie Cheesecake Bites
- Chocolate-Dipped Strawberries
- Cottage Cheese with Pineapple
- Strawberry Banana Smoothie
- Almond Flour Cookies
- Frozen Grapes
- Coconut Macaroons
- Vanilla Pudding Made with Almond Milk
- Pumpkin Spice Muffins
- Peach and Raspberry Crumble
- Low-Calorie Chia Jam
- Greek Yogurt and Fruit Parfait
- Mixed Berry Compote
- Pumpkin and Cinnamon Energy Balls
- No-Bake Oatmeal Cookies
- Apple Cinnamon Chips
- Fruit-Infused Watermelon Pizza
- Almond and Date Truffles
- Light Chocolate Mousse
- Raspberry Lemonade Popsicles
- Strawberry Kiwi Salad
- Oat and Berry Bars
- Pineapple Coconut Chia Pudding
- Matcha Green Tea Ice Cream
- Caramelized Banana Slices

- Vegan Chocolate Avocado Pudding
- Cinnamon Roasted Almonds
- Blueberry Yogurt Muffins
- Fig and Walnut Energy Balls
- Low-Calorie Strawberry Shortcake
- Poppy Seed Lemon Cake
- Dark Chocolate-Covered Banana Bites
- Orange and Almond Cake
- Spiced Pear Compote
- Strawberry Coconut Chia Bars
- Peach and Yogurt Smoothie
- Berry and Almond Crumble
- Lemon Zest Energy Bites
- Frozen Yogurt Bark with Fruit

Greek Yogurt with Honey and Berries

Ingredients:

- 1 cup Greek yogurt (plain, non-fat or low-fat)
- 1 tablespoon honey
- 1/2 cup mixed berries (e.g., strawberries, blueberries, raspberries)

Instructions:

1. **Prepare the Yogurt:** Spoon the Greek yogurt into a bowl.
2. **Add Honey:** Drizzle the honey over the yogurt.
3. **Top with Berries:** Scatter the mixed berries on top of the yogurt and honey.
4. **Serve:** Enjoy immediately or chill for a cooler treat.

Optional: Garnish with a sprinkle of granola or a few mint leaves for extra flavor.

Baked Apples with Cinnamon

Ingredients:

- 4 large apples (e.g., Granny Smith or Honeycrisp)
- 1/4 cup chopped nuts (e.g., walnuts, pecans) – optional
- 1/4 cup raisins or dried cranberries – optional
- 1 tablespoon honey or maple syrup
- 1 teaspoon ground cinnamon
- 1/4 teaspoon ground nutmeg
- 1/4 cup water

Instructions:

1. **Preheat Oven:** Preheat your oven to 350°F (175°C).
2. **Prepare Apples:** Core the apples using an apple corer or a paring knife, making a large enough cavity to hold the filling.
3. **Mix Filling:** In a small bowl, mix the chopped nuts, raisins or dried cranberries, honey or maple syrup, cinnamon, and nutmeg.
4. **Stuff Apples:** Spoon the filling mixture into the cavity of each apple.
5. **Bake:** Place the apples in a baking dish and pour the water into the bottom of the dish to help keep the apples moist.
6. **Bake Apples:** Cover the dish with aluminum foil and bake for 25-30 minutes, or until the apples are tender when pierced with a fork.
7. **Serve:** Let the apples cool slightly before serving. Enjoy warm.

Optional: Top with a dollop of Greek yogurt or a sprinkle of extra cinnamon if desired.

Chia Seed Pudding

Ingredients:

- 1/4 cup chia seeds
- 1 cup almond milk (or any milk of your choice)
- 1-2 tablespoons honey or maple syrup (adjust to taste)
- 1/2 teaspoon vanilla extract

Instructions:

1. **Mix Ingredients:** In a bowl or jar, combine chia seeds, almond milk, honey (or maple syrup), and vanilla extract. Stir well to combine.
2. **Let Sit:** Allow the mixture to sit for 5 minutes, then stir again to prevent clumping.
3. **Refrigerate:** Cover and refrigerate for at least 2 hours or overnight. The chia seeds will absorb the liquid and thicken into a pudding-like consistency.
4. **Serve:** Stir the pudding before serving. You can top with fresh fruit, nuts, or a sprinkle of cinnamon if desired.

Optional: For added flavor, try incorporating cocoa powder, fruit purees, or a pinch of sea salt.

Banana Ice Cream

Ingredients:

- 4 ripe bananas

Instructions:

1. **Prepare Bananas:** Peel the bananas and slice them into thin rounds.
2. **Freeze Bananas:** Place the banana slices in a single layer on a baking sheet or plate and freeze until solid, about 2 hours.
3. **Blend:** Transfer the frozen banana slices to a food processor or high-speed blender. Blend until smooth and creamy, stopping to scrape down the sides as needed.
4. **Serve:** Scoop the banana ice cream into bowls and enjoy immediately. For a firmer texture, you can freeze the blended mixture for an additional 30 minutes before serving.

Optional: Add-ins like a splash of vanilla extract, a tablespoon of cocoa powder, or a handful of berries can be blended in for extra flavor.

Berry Sorbet

Ingredients:

- 2 cups mixed berries (e.g., strawberries, blueberries, raspberries, blackberries)
- 1/2 cup honey or maple syrup (adjust to taste)
- 1/4 cup water or lemon juice (for extra tartness)
- 1 tablespoon lemon juice (optional, for added flavor)

Instructions:

1. **Prepare Berries:** If using fresh berries, wash them thoroughly. If using frozen berries, there's no need to thaw them.
2. **Blend:** In a blender or food processor, combine the berries, honey or maple syrup, and lemon juice (if using). Blend until smooth.
3. **Adjust Consistency:** Add water or additional lemon juice as needed to reach your desired consistency. If the mixture is too thick, add a bit more water or lemon juice.
4. **Freeze:** Pour the berry mixture into a shallow dish or ice cream maker. If using a dish, freeze for about 2 hours, stirring every 30 minutes to break up any ice crystals.
5. **Serve:** Once the sorbet is firm and has a fluffy texture, scoop it into bowls and serve.

Optional: Garnish with fresh mint leaves or a few extra berries for an elegant touch.

Mango Coconut Popsicles

Ingredients:

- 2 cups ripe mango chunks (fresh or frozen)
- 1 cup coconut milk (canned, full-fat or light)
- 2 tablespoons honey or maple syrup (adjust to taste)
- 1 teaspoon lime juice (optional, for a hint of tartness)

Instructions:

1. **Blend Ingredients:** In a blender, combine the mango chunks, coconut milk, honey (or maple syrup), and lime juice (if using). Blend until smooth and creamy.
2. **Pour into Molds:** Pour the mixture into popsicle molds, leaving a little space at the top for expansion.
3. **Insert Sticks:** Place popsicle sticks into the molds.
4. **Freeze:** Freeze for at least 4 hours, or until completely frozen.
5. **Unmold and Serve:** To release the popsicles, run warm water briefly over the outside of the molds or gently pull on the sticks. Enjoy immediately!

Optional: For added texture, you can stir in some shredded coconut or small chunks of mango before freezing.

Fruit Salad with Mint

Ingredients:

- 2 cups strawberries, hulled and quartered
- 1 cup blueberries
- 1 cup diced pineapple
- 1 cup diced mango
- 1 cup seedless cucumber, diced (optional, for extra crunch)
- 1-2 tablespoons honey or agave syrup (optional, to taste)
- 2 tablespoons fresh mint leaves, finely chopped
- Juice of 1 lime

Instructions:

1. **Prepare Fruit:** Wash and prepare the fruit as indicated. Place all the fruit into a large bowl.
2. **Add Sweetener:** If desired, drizzle honey or agave syrup over the fruit for added sweetness. Gently toss to combine.
3. **Add Mint and Lime Juice:** Sprinkle the chopped mint leaves over the fruit and squeeze the lime juice on top.
4. **Toss and Serve:** Gently toss the fruit salad to mix everything evenly. Serve immediately or refrigerate for up to 2 hours before serving.

Optional: For an extra burst of flavor, you can add a sprinkle of chia seeds or a handful of toasted nuts.

Light Lemon Bars

Ingredients:

For the Crust:

- 1 cup almond flour
- 2 tablespoons coconut oil or unsalted butter, melted
- 2 tablespoons honey or maple syrup
- 1/4 teaspoon salt

For the Lemon Filling:

- 1/2 cup lemon juice (about 2-3 lemons)
- 1/4 cup honey or maple syrup
- 3 large eggs
- 1 tablespoon lemon zest
- 1 tablespoon all-purpose flour or cornstarch
- Powdered sugar for dusting (optional)

Instructions:

1. **Preheat Oven:** Preheat your oven to 350°F (175°C). Line an 8x8-inch baking pan with parchment paper, leaving a slight overhang for easy removal.
2. **Make the Crust:**
    - In a medium bowl, combine the almond flour, melted coconut oil (or butter), honey (or maple syrup), and salt. Mix until well combined.
    - Press the mixture evenly into the bottom of the prepared pan.
    - Bake for 10-12 minutes, or until lightly golden. Remove from the oven and let cool slightly.
3. **Prepare the Lemon Filling:**
    - In a medium bowl, whisk together the lemon juice, honey (or maple syrup), eggs, lemon zest, and flour (or cornstarch) until smooth and well combined.
    - Pour the filling over the pre-baked crust.
4. **Bake Bars:**
    - Bake for 18-20 minutes, or until the filling is set and the edges are slightly golden.
    - Let the bars cool completely in the pan on a wire rack.
5. **Serve:**
    - Once cooled, lift the bars out of the pan using the parchment paper overhang.
    - Cut into squares and dust with powdered sugar, if desired.

Optional: Garnish with additional lemon zest or fresh mint leaves for extra flavor and visual appeal.

Apple Nachos

Ingredients:

- 2 large apples (e.g., Granny Smith, Honeycrisp)
- 2 tablespoons almond butter or peanut butter
- 1 tablespoon honey or maple syrup
- 2 tablespoons granola
- 2 tablespoons mini dark chocolate chips or cacao nibs (optional)
- 1 tablespoon chopped nuts (e.g., almonds, walnuts) – optional
- 1/2 teaspoon cinnamon (optional)
- Fresh fruit or dried fruit (e.g., raisins, dried cranberries) – optional

Instructions:

1. **Prepare Apples:**
   - Wash and core the apples. Slice them into thin rounds or wedges, about 1/4 inch thick. You can use a mandoline for uniform slices if you have one.
2. **Arrange Apple Slices:**
   - Lay the apple slices in a single layer on a serving plate or platter.
3. **Add Toppings:**
   - In a small bowl, mix the almond butter (or peanut butter) with the honey (or maple syrup) until smooth. Drizzle this mixture over the apple slices.
   - Sprinkle granola evenly over the apples.
   - Add mini dark chocolate chips or cacao nibs, if using.
   - If desired, sprinkle chopped nuts and a dash of cinnamon over the top.
4. **Add Extra Toppings:**
   - For additional flavor, you can add a handful of fresh fruit or a sprinkle of dried fruit.
5. **Serve:**
   - Serve immediately and enjoy as a fun and healthy snack or dessert.

Optional: For a bit more crunch, you can lightly toast the granola or nuts before adding them.

Watermelon Slush

Ingredients:

- 4 cups seedless watermelon chunks (fresh or frozen)
- 1 tablespoon lime juice (about 1 lime)
- 1-2 tablespoons honey or maple syrup (adjust to taste)
- 1/2 cup cold water or coconut water (optional, for desired consistency)
- Fresh mint leaves for garnish (optional)

Instructions:

1. **Prepare Watermelon:**
    - If using fresh watermelon, cut it into chunks and remove any seeds. For a colder slush, you can freeze the watermelon chunks for a few hours or overnight.
2. **Blend Ingredients:**
    - In a blender, combine the watermelon chunks, lime juice, and honey (or maple syrup). Blend until smooth.
    - If the mixture is too thick, add cold water or coconut water a little at a time until you reach your desired consistency.
3. **Serve:**
    - Pour the watermelon slush into glasses. Garnish with fresh mint leaves if desired.
4. **Optional:**
    - For an extra twist, you can add a splash of sparkling water just before serving for a fizzy version.

Note: If you prefer a more frozen texture, blend the slush for a longer time or use frozen watermelon chunks.

Baked Pears with Almonds

Ingredients:

- 4 ripe but firm pears (e.g., Bosc, Anjou)
- 1/4 cup sliced almonds
- 2 tablespoons honey or maple syrup
- 1 teaspoon ground cinnamon
- 1/4 teaspoon ground nutmeg (optional)
- 1/4 cup water
- Fresh mint leaves for garnish (optional)

Instructions:

1. **Preheat Oven:** Preheat your oven to 350°F (175°C).
2. **Prepare Pears:**
   - Wash and halve the pears. Remove the core and seeds using a melon baller or a small spoon.
3. **Arrange Pears:**
   - Place the pear halves cut-side up in a baking dish.
4. **Add Toppings:**
   - Drizzle honey or maple syrup evenly over the pears.
   - Sprinkle the ground cinnamon and nutmeg (if using) over the pears.
   - Scatter the sliced almonds on top of each pear half.
5. **Add Water:**
   - Pour the water into the bottom of the baking dish to help keep the pears moist during baking.
6. **Bake:**
   - Bake for 20-25 minutes, or until the pears are tender when pierced with a fork and the almonds are golden brown.
7. **Serve:**
   - Allow the pears to cool slightly before serving. Garnish with fresh mint leaves if desired.

Optional: Serve with a dollop of Greek yogurt or a scoop of vanilla ice cream for an extra treat.

Low-Calorie Cheesecake Bites

Ingredients:

- 1 cup low-fat cream cheese (softened)
- 1/2 cup Greek yogurt (plain, non-fat)
- 1/4 cup honey or maple syrup
- 1 teaspoon vanilla extract
- 1 tablespoon lemon juice (optional, for added tang)
- Fresh berries or fruit for topping (optional)

Instructions:

1. **Prepare Ingredients:**
    - In a mixing bowl, combine the softened cream cheese, Greek yogurt, honey (or maple syrup), vanilla extract, and lemon juice (if using).
2. **Mix:**
    - Use an electric mixer or whisk to blend the ingredients until smooth and creamy.
3. **Chill Mixture:**
    - Refrigerate the mixture for about 30 minutes to firm up slightly.
4. **Form Bites:**
    - Once chilled, use a small cookie scoop or a teaspoon to form bite-sized portions of the cheesecake mixture. Place them on a parchment-lined tray or plate.
5. **Chill Again:**
    - Refrigerate the bites for another 30 minutes to an hour, allowing them to firm up.
6. **Serve:**
    - Just before serving, top each cheesecake bite with a fresh berry or a small piece of fruit if desired.

Optional: For a touch of added flavor, you can sprinkle a little graham cracker crumb or a tiny bit of shredded coconut on top of each bite before serving.

Enjoy these light and creamy cheesecake bites as a guilt-free treat!

Chocolate-Dipped Strawberries

Ingredients:

- 1 pint fresh strawberries (with stems)
- 1 cup dark chocolate chips or chopped dark chocolate (70% cocoa or higher for a lower-calorie option)
- 1 tablespoon coconut oil (optional, for smoother melting)

Instructions:

1. **Prepare Strawberries:**
   - Wash the strawberries and gently pat them dry with paper towels. Ensure they are completely dry to help the chocolate adhere.
2. **Melt Chocolate:**
   - In a microwave-safe bowl, combine the chocolate chips and coconut oil (if using).
   - Microwave in 20-30 second intervals, stirring between each interval until the chocolate is fully melted and smooth. Alternatively, melt the chocolate using a double boiler on the stove.
3. **Dip Strawberries:**
   - Hold each strawberry by the stem and dip it into the melted chocolate, covering about 2/3 of the berry. Gently shake off any excess chocolate.
4. **Cool:**
   - Place the dipped strawberries on a parchment-lined tray or plate.
   - Refrigerate for about 15-30 minutes, or until the chocolate is set.
5. **Serve:**
   - Serve chilled or at room temperature. Enjoy!

Optional: For added flair, you can drizzle the dipped strawberries with a different type of chocolate (e.g., white chocolate) or sprinkle with finely chopped nuts or a dash of sea salt before the chocolate sets.

Cottage Cheese with Pineapple

Ingredients:

- 1 cup low-fat or non-fat cottage cheese
- 1/2 cup pineapple chunks (fresh or canned in juice, not syrup)
- 1 tablespoon honey or maple syrup (optional, for added sweetness)
- A few fresh mint leaves for garnish (optional)

Instructions:

1. **Prepare Pineapple:**
    - If using fresh pineapple, peel and cut it into chunks. If using canned pineapple, drain it well to remove excess liquid.
2. **Combine Ingredients:**
    - In a bowl, mix the cottage cheese with the pineapple chunks.
3. **Add Sweetener (Optional):**
    - If you prefer a sweeter taste, drizzle the honey or maple syrup over the mixture and stir to combine.
4. **Garnish and Serve:**
    - Garnish with fresh mint leaves if desired. Serve immediately or chill in the refrigerator until ready to eat.

Optional: For added texture, you can sprinkle a few toasted coconut flakes or a handful of granola on top before serving.

Strawberry Banana Smoothie

Ingredients:

- 1 cup fresh or frozen strawberries
- 1 ripe banana
- 1/2 cup Greek yogurt (plain or vanilla, non-fat or low-fat)
- 1/2 cup almond milk (or any milk of your choice)
- 1 tablespoon honey or maple syrup (optional, for added sweetness)
- 1/2 teaspoon vanilla extract (optional)
- A few ice cubes (if using fresh strawberries and you want a thicker, colder smoothie)

Instructions:

1. **Prepare Ingredients:**
    - If using fresh strawberries, wash and hull them. Peel the banana.
2. **Blend:**
    - In a blender, combine the strawberries, banana, Greek yogurt, and almond milk.
    - Add honey or maple syrup and vanilla extract if using.
    - Blend until smooth and creamy. If the smoothie is too thick, you can add a bit more almond milk to reach your desired consistency.
3. **Add Ice (Optional):**
    - If using fresh strawberries and want a colder, thicker smoothie, add a few ice cubes and blend again until well incorporated.
4. **Serve:**
    - Pour the smoothie into glasses and enjoy immediately.

Optional: You can also add a handful of spinach for a nutrient boost or a tablespoon of chia seeds for extra fiber.

Almond Flour Cookies

Ingredients:

- 2 cups almond flour
- 1/4 cup honey or maple syrup
- 1/4 cup coconut oil or unsalted butter, melted
- 1 large egg
- 1/2 teaspoon vanilla extract
- 1/4 teaspoon baking soda
- 1/4 teaspoon salt
- Optional: 1/4 cup mini chocolate chips or chopped nuts

Instructions:

1. **Preheat Oven:**
   - Preheat your oven to 350°F (175°C). Line a baking sheet with parchment paper.
2. **Mix Wet Ingredients:**
   - In a large bowl, whisk together the melted coconut oil (or butter), honey (or maple syrup), egg, and vanilla extract.
3. **Combine Dry Ingredients:**
   - In another bowl, mix the almond flour, baking soda, and salt.
4. **Combine Wet and Dry:**
   - Add the dry ingredients to the wet ingredients and mix until well combined. If using, fold in the mini chocolate chips or chopped nuts.
5. **Shape Cookies:**
   - Scoop tablespoon-sized balls of dough onto the prepared baking sheet. Flatten them slightly with the back of a spoon or your fingers.
6. **Bake:**
   - Bake for 10-12 minutes, or until the edges are golden brown. The cookies will firm up as they cool.
7. **Cool:**
   - Let the cookies cool on the baking sheet for 5 minutes before transferring them to a wire rack to cool completely.

Optional: For added flavor, you can sprinkle a pinch of sea salt on top of each cookie before baking or drizzle with a bit of melted dark chocolate once they've cooled.

Frozen Grapes

Ingredients:

- 2 cups seedless grapes (any variety)

Instructions:

1. **Wash and Dry Grapes:**
   - Wash the grapes thoroughly under cold water to remove any dirt or residue.
   - Pat them dry with a clean towel to ensure they freeze properly.
2. **Prepare for Freezing:**
   - Remove the grapes from the stems and place them in a single layer on a baking sheet or plate lined with parchment paper. This prevents them from sticking together during freezing.
3. **Freeze Grapes:**
   - Place the baking sheet or plate in the freezer.
   - Freeze the grapes for at least 2-3 hours or until they are solid.
4. **Store:**
   - Once frozen, transfer the grapes to a resealable plastic bag or airtight container for long-term storage. They can be kept in the freezer for up to 3 months.
5. **Serve:**
   - Enjoy the frozen grapes as a refreshing snack straight from the freezer. They're great on their own or can be added to smoothies or as a chilled topping for yogurt.

Optional: For a twist, you can roll the grapes in a small amount of cinnamon before freezing, or drizzle with a bit of honey and let it set before freezing.

Coconut Macaroons

Ingredients:

- 2 1/2 cups shredded coconut (unsweetened or sweetened, depending on your preference)
- 1/2 cup sweetened condensed milk
- 1/4 teaspoon vanilla extract
- 1 large egg white
- 1/4 teaspoon salt
- Optional: 1/2 cup dark chocolate chips (for dipping)

Instructions:

1. **Preheat Oven:**
   - Preheat your oven to 325°F (165°C). Line a baking sheet with parchment paper or a silicone baking mat.
2. **Mix Ingredients:**
   - In a large bowl, combine the shredded coconut, sweetened condensed milk, and vanilla extract. Stir until well mixed.
3. **Whip Egg White:**
   - In a separate bowl, beat the egg white with a pinch of salt until stiff peaks form. This can be done with an electric mixer or a whisk.
4. **Combine:**
   - Gently fold the whipped egg white into the coconut mixture until well combined. Be careful not to deflate the egg white too much.
5. **Form Macaroons:**
   - Using a small cookie scoop or spoon, drop rounded mounds of the mixture onto the prepared baking sheet. Space them about 1 inch apart.
6. **Bake:**
   - Bake for 15-20 minutes, or until the macaroons are golden brown around the edges.
7. **Cool:**
   - Allow the macaroons to cool on the baking sheet for 10 minutes before transferring them to a wire rack to cool completely.
8. **Optional Chocolate Dip:**
   - If desired, melt the dark chocolate chips in a microwave-safe bowl or using a double boiler. Dip the bottom of each macaroon into the melted chocolate and place them back on the parchment-lined baking sheet. Let the chocolate set before serving.

Storage: Store the macaroons in an airtight container at room temperature for up to a week, or in the refrigerator for longer freshness.

Vanilla Pudding Made with Almond Milk

Ingredients:

- 2 1/2 cups unsweetened almond milk
- 1/2 cup granulated sugar (or a low-calorie sweetener of your choice)
- 1/4 cup cornstarch
- 1/4 teaspoon salt
- 1 tablespoon unsalted butter or a dairy-free alternative
- 1 teaspoon vanilla extract

Instructions:

1. **Mix Dry Ingredients:**
   - In a medium saucepan, whisk together the sugar, cornstarch, and salt.
2. **Add Almond Milk:**
   - Gradually whisk in the almond milk to ensure there are no lumps.
3. **Cook Mixture:**
   - Place the saucepan over medium heat. Cook the mixture, stirring constantly, until it begins to thicken and comes to a gentle boil. This usually takes about 5-7 minutes.
4. **Simmer:**
   - Once the pudding has thickened, reduce the heat to low and continue to cook for another 1-2 minutes, stirring frequently.
5. **Remove from Heat:**
   - Remove the saucepan from heat. Stir in the butter and vanilla extract until the butter is melted and fully incorporated.
6. **Cool and Serve:**
   - Transfer the pudding to individual serving dishes or a large bowl. Allow it to cool to room temperature. Once cooled, you can cover and refrigerate for at least 2 hours to fully set.
7. **Optional Garnish:**
   - Before serving, you can top the pudding with fresh fruit, a sprinkle of cinnamon, or a dollop of dairy-free whipped cream if desired.

Storage: Store any leftovers in an airtight container in the refrigerator for up to 3 days.

Enjoy this smooth and creamy vanilla pudding as a comforting dessert or snack!

Pumpkin Spice Muffins

Ingredients:

- 1 1/2 cups whole wheat flour (or all-purpose flour)
- 1 teaspoon baking powder
- 1/2 teaspoon baking soda
- 1/2 teaspoon salt
- 1 teaspoon ground cinnamon
- 1/2 teaspoon ground nutmeg
- 1/4 teaspoon ground ginger
- 1/2 cup pumpkin puree (canned or homemade)
- 1/2 cup Greek yogurt (plain, non-fat or low-fat)
- 1/4 cup honey or maple syrup
- 1/4 cup unsweetened applesauce
- 1 large egg
- 1 teaspoon vanilla extract
- Optional: 1/4 cup chopped nuts or dark chocolate chips for added texture

Instructions:

1. **Preheat Oven:**
   - Preheat your oven to 350°F (175°C). Line a muffin tin with paper liners or lightly grease the cups.
2. **Mix Dry Ingredients:**
   - In a medium bowl, whisk together the flour, baking powder, baking soda, salt, cinnamon, nutmeg, and ginger.
3. **Mix Wet Ingredients:**
   - In a large bowl, combine the pumpkin puree, Greek yogurt, honey (or maple syrup), applesauce, egg, and vanilla extract. Mix until well combined.
4. **Combine Mixtures:**
   - Gradually add the dry ingredients to the wet ingredients, stirring just until combined. Be careful not to overmix.
5. **Add Optional Ingredients:**
   - If using, gently fold in the chopped nuts or dark chocolate chips.
6. **Fill Muffin Cups:**
   - Divide the batter evenly among the muffin cups, filling each about 2/3 full.
7. **Bake:**
   - Bake for 18-22 minutes, or until a toothpick inserted into the center of a muffin comes out clean.
8. **Cool:**
   - Allow the muffins to cool in the tin for 5 minutes before transferring them to a wire rack to cool completely.

Optional Glaze:

- For a simple glaze, mix a tablespoon of powdered sugar with a few teaspoons of milk until smooth and drizzle over the cooled muffins.

Enjoy these moist and spiced pumpkin muffins as a snack or breakfast treat!

Peach and Raspberry Crumble

Ingredients:

For the Filling:

- 4 cups fresh or frozen peaches (peeled and sliced)
- 1 cup fresh raspberries
- 1/4 cup granulated sugar (adjust to taste)
- 1 tablespoon cornstarch
- 1 tablespoon lemon juice
- 1/2 teaspoon vanilla extract

For the Crumble Topping:

- 1 cup rolled oats
- 1/2 cup almond flour (or all-purpose flour)
- 1/2 cup brown sugar (or coconut sugar for a lower-calorie option)
- 1/4 teaspoon ground cinnamon
- 1/4 cup unsalted butter or coconut oil, melted
- A pinch of salt

Instructions:

1. **Preheat Oven:**
   - Preheat your oven to 350°F (175°C).
2. **Prepare the Filling:**
   - In a large bowl, combine the peaches, raspberries, sugar, cornstarch, lemon juice, and vanilla extract. Gently mix until the fruit is evenly coated.
3. **Transfer Filling:**
   - Pour the fruit mixture into a baking dish (about 8x8 inches or similar).
4. **Make the Crumble Topping:**
   - In a separate bowl, mix together the rolled oats, almond flour, brown sugar, ground cinnamon, melted butter (or coconut oil), and a pinch of salt. Stir until the mixture is well combined and crumbly.
5. **Top the Fruit:**
   - Sprinkle the crumble topping evenly over the fruit filling.
6. **Bake:**
   - Bake in the preheated oven for 35-40 minutes, or until the topping is golden brown and the filling is bubbling.
7. **Cool:**
   - Allow the crumble to cool slightly before serving. This lets the juices set a bit and makes it easier to serve.

Serving Suggestions:

- Enjoy warm on its own or with a scoop of vanilla ice cream or a dollop of Greek yogurt for a delightful dessert.

Storage:

- Store any leftovers in an airtight container in the refrigerator for up to 4 days. Reheat in the oven or microwave before serving.

This Peach and Raspberry Crumble is a perfect blend of sweet and tart flavors with a crispy, buttery topping. Enjoy!

Low-Calorie Chia Jam

Ingredients:

- 2 cups fresh or frozen fruit (e.g., berries, peaches, or apricots)
- 2 tablespoons chia seeds
- 1-2 tablespoons honey or maple syrup (adjust to taste)
- 1 tablespoon lemon juice
- Optional: 1/2 teaspoon vanilla extract or a pinch of ground cinnamon for extra flavor

Instructions:

1. **Prepare Fruit:**
   - If using fresh fruit, wash and chop it into small pieces. If using frozen fruit, thaw it slightly.
2. **Cook Fruit:**
   - In a medium saucepan, combine the fruit and lemon juice. Cook over medium heat, stirring occasionally, until the fruit breaks down and becomes saucy (about 5-10 minutes). If you prefer a smoother texture, use a fork or potato masher to mash the fruit as it cooks.
3. **Add Sweetener:**
   - Stir in the honey or maple syrup. Adjust the sweetness to your taste.
4. **Add Chia Seeds:**
   - Stir in the chia seeds and continue to cook for another 2-3 minutes, until the mixture starts to thicken.
5. **Cool:**
   - Remove from heat and let the jam cool to room temperature. It will continue to thicken as it cools.
6. **Optional Flavorings:**
   - If desired, stir in vanilla extract or ground cinnamon once the jam has cooled slightly.
7. **Store:**
   - Transfer the chia jam to a clean jar or airtight container. Store in the refrigerator for up to 1-2 weeks.

Serving Suggestions:

- Enjoy the chia jam on toast, yogurt, oatmeal, or as a filling for baked goods. It's a versatile and low-calorie option for adding natural sweetness and flavor to your meals.

This chia jam is easy to make and can be customized with your favorite fruits and flavorings.

Greek Yogurt and Fruit Parfait

Ingredients:

- 1 cup plain Greek yogurt (non-fat or low-fat)
- 1 tablespoon honey or maple syrup (optional, for added sweetness)
- 1/2 teaspoon vanilla extract (optional)
- 1 cup mixed fresh fruit (e.g., berries, sliced bananas, diced apples, or peaches)
- 1/4 cup granola
- A few fresh mint leaves for garnish (optional)

Instructions:

1. **Prepare Yogurt:**
   - In a bowl, mix the Greek yogurt with honey or maple syrup and vanilla extract if using. Stir until smooth and well combined.
2. **Prepare Fruit:**
   - Wash and chop the fresh fruit into bite-sized pieces.
3. **Assemble Parfait:**
   - In serving glasses or bowls, start by layering a spoonful of Greek yogurt at the bottom.
   - Add a layer of fresh fruit on top of the yogurt.
   - Sprinkle a layer of granola over the fruit.
4. **Repeat Layers:**
   - Add another layer of Greek yogurt, followed by more fruit and granola. Continue layering until the glass or bowl is filled, finishing with a layer of granola on top.
5. **Garnish (Optional):**
   - Garnish with fresh mint leaves if desired.
6. **Serve:**
   - Serve immediately or chill in the refrigerator for up to 2 hours before serving.

Optional Variations:

- **For added flavor:** Mix in a sprinkle of cinnamon or nutmeg with the yogurt.
- **For extra crunch:** Top with nuts, seeds, or a drizzle of nut butter.
- **For more protein:** Add a scoop of protein powder to the Greek yogurt.

Enjoy this Greek Yogurt and Fruit Parfait as a healthy breakfast, snack, or dessert!

Mixed Berry Compote

Ingredients:

- 2 cups mixed berries (fresh or frozen, e.g., strawberries, blueberries, raspberries, blackberries)
- 1/4 cup granulated sugar or maple syrup (adjust to taste)
- 1 tablespoon lemon juice
- 1/2 teaspoon vanilla extract (optional)
- 1/2 teaspoon cornstarch mixed with 1 tablespoon water (optional, for thickening)

Instructions:

1. **Prepare Berries:**
    - If using fresh berries, rinse them gently and pat dry. If using frozen berries, there's no need to thaw them beforehand.
2. **Cook Compote:**
    - In a medium saucepan, combine the berries, sugar or maple syrup, and lemon juice.
    - Cook over medium heat, stirring occasionally, until the berries start to break down and the mixture becomes syrupy (about 5-10 minutes).
3. **Thicken (Optional):**
    - If you prefer a thicker compote, mix the cornstarch with water to create a slurry. Stir the slurry into the berry mixture and cook for an additional 1-2 minutes, or until the compote reaches your desired thickness.
4. **Add Flavor (Optional):**
    - Stir in vanilla extract, if using.
5. **Cool:**
    - Remove the compote from heat and let it cool to room temperature. It will thicken slightly as it cools.
6. **Serve:**
    - Serve the compote warm or chilled over yogurt, oatmeal, pancakes, waffles, or as a topping for desserts.

Storage:

- Store any leftovers in an airtight container in the refrigerator for up to 1 week. The compote can also be frozen for up to 3 months.

This Mixed Berry Compote is versatile and can be customized with your favorite berries or a touch of spice. Enjoy!

Pumpkin and Cinnamon Energy Balls

Ingredients:

- 1 cup rolled oats
- 1/2 cup canned pumpkin puree (not pumpkin pie filling)
- 1/4 cup almond butter or peanut butter
- 1/4 cup honey or maple syrup
- 1/2 teaspoon ground cinnamon
- 1/4 teaspoon ground nutmeg
- 1/4 teaspoon vanilla extract
- 1/4 cup mini chocolate chips or chopped nuts (optional)
- A pinch of salt

Instructions:

1. **Combine Ingredients:**
   - In a large bowl, mix together the rolled oats, pumpkin puree, almond butter (or peanut butter), honey (or maple syrup), ground cinnamon, ground nutmeg, and vanilla extract. Stir until well combined.
2. **Add Optional Ingredients:**
   - If using, fold in the mini chocolate chips or chopped nuts for added texture and flavor.
3. **Chill Mixture:**
   - Refrigerate the mixture for about 30 minutes. This helps it firm up and makes it easier to roll into balls.
4. **Form Energy Balls:**
   - Once chilled, use your hands or a small cookie scoop to form the mixture into bite-sized balls, about 1 inch in diameter.
5. **Store:**
   - Place the energy balls in an airtight container. Store in the refrigerator for up to 1 week, or in the freezer for up to 3 months.

Optional Coating:

- For a touch of extra flavor or texture, roll the energy balls in a bit of extra ground cinnamon or shredded coconut before storing.

These Pumpkin and Cinnamon Energy Balls are perfect for a quick snack or a healthy treat and are packed with nutrients and flavor. Enjoy!

No-Bake Oatmeal Cookies

Ingredients:

- 1 cup rolled oats
- 1/2 cup creamy peanut butter (or almond butter for a different flavor)
- 1/2 cup honey or maple syrup
- 1/4 cup unsweetened cocoa powder (optional, for chocolate flavor)
- 1/4 cup mini chocolate chips or raisins (optional)
- 1/2 teaspoon vanilla extract
- A pinch of salt

Instructions:

1. **Prepare Ingredients:**
   - In a medium saucepan, combine the honey (or maple syrup) and peanut butter. Heat over medium heat, stirring occasionally, until the mixture is smooth and just starts to boil.
2. **Add Cocoa Powder (Optional):**
   - If you're making chocolate cookies, stir in the unsweetened cocoa powder until fully incorporated.
3. **Combine with Oats:**
   - Remove the saucepan from heat and stir in the vanilla extract and a pinch of salt.
   - Add the rolled oats and mix until the oats are well coated with the mixture.
4. **Add Mix-Ins (Optional):**
   - Fold in the mini chocolate chips or raisins if using.
5. **Shape Cookies:**
   - Drop spoonfuls of the mixture onto a baking sheet lined with parchment paper or wax paper. Flatten each cookie slightly with the back of a spoon.
6. **Cool:**
   - Let the cookies cool at room temperature until they set. This usually takes about 30 minutes. If you're in a hurry, you can refrigerate them to speed up the setting process.

Storage:

- Store the no-bake oatmeal cookies in an airtight container at room temperature for up to 1 week, or in the refrigerator for up to 2 weeks. They can also be frozen for up to 3 months.

These no-bake oatmeal cookies are perfect for a quick treat or snack and are highly customizable with your favorite add-ins!

Apple Cinnamon Chips

Ingredients:

- 2 large apples (e.g., Fuji, Honeycrisp, or any sweet variety)
- 1 tablespoon lemon juice
- 1 tablespoon granulated sugar or coconut sugar
- 1/2 teaspoon ground cinnamon

Instructions:

1. **Preheat Oven:**
    - Preheat your oven to 225°F (110°C). Line a baking sheet with parchment paper.
2. **Prepare Apples:**
    - Wash and core the apples. Using a mandolin slicer or a sharp knife, slice the apples as thinly as possible, about 1/8 inch thick. The thinner the slices, the crispier the chips will be.
3. **Toss with Lemon Juice:**
    - In a large bowl, toss the apple slices with lemon juice to prevent browning.
4. **Mix Sugar and Cinnamon:**
    - In a small bowl, combine the granulated sugar (or coconut sugar) and ground cinnamon.
5. **Coat Apple Slices:**
    - Arrange the apple slices in a single layer on the prepared baking sheet. Sprinkle the cinnamon sugar mixture evenly over the slices.
6. **Bake:**
    - Bake in the preheated oven for 1.5 to 2 hours, flipping the slices halfway through baking. The chips are done when they are dry and crispy but not burned. Keep an eye on them in the last 30 minutes to avoid overcooking.
7. **Cool:**
    - Allow the apple chips to cool completely on the baking sheet. They will become crispier as they cool.
8. **Store:**
    - Store the cooled apple cinnamon chips in an airtight container at room temperature for up to 1 week.

Optional: For added flavor, you can sprinkle a bit of sea salt on the apple slices before baking or experiment with other spices like nutmeg or cardamom.

Enjoy these crunchy and flavorful apple cinnamon chips as a healthy snack or a crunchy topping for yogurt or salads!

Fruit-Infused Watermelon Pizza

Ingredients:

- 1 small to medium-sized seedless watermelon
- 1 cup fresh berries (e.g., strawberries, blueberries, raspberries, blackberries)
- 1 kiwi, peeled and sliced
- 1/2 cup sliced grapes (red or green)
- 1/2 cup pineapple chunks (fresh or canned, drained)
- Fresh mint leaves for garnish (optional)
- 1 tablespoon honey or agave syrup (optional, for drizzling)

Instructions:

1. **Prepare Watermelon:**
   - Slice the watermelon into 1/2-inch thick rounds. Remove any seeds if necessary.
   - Cut each round into "pizza slices" by cutting it into wedges.
2. **Arrange Toppings:**
   - Place the watermelon slices on a large platter or cutting board.
   - Arrange the fresh berries, kiwi slices, grapes, and pineapple chunks on top of the watermelon slices in a decorative pattern.
3. **Add Optional Drizzle:**
   - If desired, drizzle a little honey or agave syrup over the fruit-topped watermelon slices for extra sweetness.
4. **Garnish:**
   - Garnish with fresh mint leaves for a touch of color and added freshness.
5. **Serve:**
   - Serve immediately as a refreshing snack, light dessert, or healthy party platter.

Storage:

- If you have leftovers, store the watermelon pizza in the refrigerator, covered with plastic wrap, for up to 1 day. The fruit may release some juice, so it's best enjoyed fresh.

This Fruit-Infused Watermelon Pizza is a fun and nutritious way to enjoy a variety of fruits while staying cool and hydrated!

Almond and Date Truffles

Ingredients:

- 1 cup raw almonds
- 1 cup pitted dates (Medjool dates work best)
- 1/4 cup unsweetened cocoa powder (optional, for coating)
- 1/4 teaspoon vanilla extract
- A pinch of sea salt (optional)
- 2 tablespoons almond butter or coconut oil (optional, for added creaminess)

Instructions:

1. **Prepare Almonds:**
   - Place the almonds in a food processor and process until finely ground. Be careful not to over-process, as the almonds can turn into almond butter if processed too long.
2. **Add Dates:**
   - Add the pitted dates to the food processor. Process until the mixture begins to stick together and forms a dough-like consistency. If the mixture is too dry, add a tablespoon of almond butter or coconut oil.
3. **Add Flavor:**
   - Add the vanilla extract and a pinch of sea salt, if using. Process again until well combined.
4. **Shape Truffles:**
   - Scoop out small amounts of the mixture and roll them into bite-sized balls using your hands.
5. **Optional Coating:**
   - If desired, roll the truffles in unsweetened cocoa powder for a chocolatey touch. You can also roll them in shredded coconut, crushed nuts, or a mixture of cinnamon and sugar.
6. **Chill:**
   - Place the truffles on a parchment-lined tray or plate and refrigerate for at least 30 minutes to firm up.
7. **Store:**
   - Store the truffles in an airtight container in the refrigerator for up to 2 weeks or freeze for longer storage.

These Almond and Date Truffles are a great healthy snack or a sweet treat for any occasion!

Light Chocolate Mousse

Ingredients:

- 1 cup semi-sweet or dark chocolate chips (or chopped chocolate)
- 1 1/4 cups plain Greek yogurt (non-fat or low-fat)
- 1/2 cup whipped egg whites (about 3 large egg whites)
- 2 tablespoons honey or maple syrup (adjust to taste)
- 1 teaspoon vanilla extract
- A pinch of salt

Instructions:

1. **Melt Chocolate:**
   - In a heatproof bowl, melt the chocolate chips over a pot of simmering water (double boiler method) or in the microwave in 20-second intervals, stirring between each interval until smooth. Allow to cool slightly.
2. **Prepare Greek Yogurt:**
   - In a medium bowl, mix the Greek yogurt with honey or maple syrup and vanilla extract. Stir until smooth.
3. **Fold in Chocolate:**
   - Gently fold the melted chocolate into the yogurt mixture until fully combined. Be careful not to over-mix, as you want to keep the mousse light and airy.
4. **Whip Egg Whites:**
   - In a clean, dry bowl, use an electric mixer to whip the egg whites with a pinch of salt until stiff peaks form.
5. **Combine:**
   - Gently fold the whipped egg whites into the chocolate-yogurt mixture in thirds. Be gentle to maintain the light and airy texture.
6. **Chill:**
   - Spoon the mousse into serving dishes or glasses. Chill in the refrigerator for at least 1 hour to set.
7. **Serve:**
   - Serve chilled, and if desired, garnish with fresh berries, a dollop of whipped cream, or a sprinkle of cocoa powder.

Note: If you're concerned about using raw eggs, you can substitute the whipped egg whites with store-bought whipped topping or a whipped aquafaba (chickpea brine) for a vegan option.

This Light Chocolate Mousse is a creamy, satisfying dessert with fewer calories and a rich chocolate flavor. Enjoy!

Raspberry Lemonade Popsicles

Ingredients:

- 2 cups fresh raspberries (or frozen raspberries, thawed)
- 1 cup freshly squeezed lemon juice (about 4-6 lemons)
- 1/2 cup honey or maple syrup (adjust to taste)
- 1 1/2 cups water (or use sparkling water for a fizzy twist)
- 1/2 teaspoon lemon zest (optional, for extra flavor)
- A few fresh mint leaves for garnish (optional)

Instructions:

1. **Prepare Raspberries:**
   - In a blender or food processor, blend the raspberries until smooth. Strain the raspberry puree through a fine mesh sieve to remove the seeds, if desired.
2. **Mix Lemonade:**
   - In a large pitcher, combine the freshly squeezed lemon juice and honey (or maple syrup). Stir until the sweetener is fully dissolved.
3. **Combine Ingredients:**
   - Add the water (or sparkling water) to the lemon juice mixture. Stir well to combine. If using lemon zest, stir it in at this point.
4. **Layer Popsicles (Optional):**
   - For a layered effect, pour a small amount of raspberry puree into each popsicle mold, then add some of the lemonade mixture. Repeat layers until the molds are filled, ending with the lemonade mixture.
5. **Insert Sticks:**
   - Insert popsicle sticks into the molds. If your popsicle molds don't have built-in sticks, you can use wooden sticks or even plastic spoons.
6. **Freeze:**
   - Place the molds in the freezer and freeze for at least 4 hours, or until completely frozen.
7. **Unmold and Serve:**
   - To release the popsicles, run the outside of the molds under warm water for a few seconds to loosen them. Gently pull out the popsicles and serve.
8. **Optional Garnish:**
   - Garnish with fresh mint leaves for a refreshing touch before serving.

Storage:

- Store any leftover popsicles in an airtight container in the freezer for up to 1 month.

These Raspberry Lemonade Popsicles are perfect for a hot day and offer a tangy, sweet, and refreshing treat!

Strawberry Kiwi Salad

Ingredients:

- 2 cups fresh strawberries, hulled and sliced
- 3 ripe kiwis, peeled and sliced
- 1/4 cup fresh mint leaves, chopped (optional, for added freshness)
- 1 tablespoon honey or maple syrup (optional, for a touch of sweetness)
- 1 tablespoon lemon juice (optional, for a tangy twist)

Instructions:

1. **Prepare Fruit:**
   - Hull and slice the strawberries into thin slices.
   - Peel and slice the kiwis into thin rounds or half-moons.
2. **Combine Ingredients:**
   - In a large bowl, gently toss the sliced strawberries and kiwis together.
3. **Add Mint (Optional):**
   - If using, add the chopped fresh mint leaves to the fruit. Toss gently to distribute.
4. **Add Sweetener and Lemon Juice (Optional):**
   - If you like, drizzle honey or maple syrup and lemon juice over the fruit. Toss gently to combine.
5. **Serve:**
   - Serve immediately for the freshest taste, or refrigerate for up to 1 hour before serving.

Tips:

- **For added texture:** Sprinkle with a small handful of nuts or seeds, like almonds or chia seeds, right before serving.
- **For extra flavor:** You can also add a sprinkle of a light herb like basil or a touch of ground cinnamon for a unique twist.

This Strawberry Kiwi Salad is light, refreshing, and perfect as a side dish or a healthy snack!

Oat and Berry Bars

Ingredients:

For the Crust and Topping:

- 1 1/2 cups rolled oats
- 1/2 cup almond flour (or all-purpose flour)
- 1/4 cup honey or maple syrup
- 1/4 cup coconut oil or unsalted butter, melted
- 1/4 cup brown sugar or coconut sugar (optional, for added sweetness)
- 1/4 teaspoon salt
- 1/2 teaspoon ground cinnamon (optional)

For the Berry Filling:

- 2 cups mixed berries (fresh or frozen; e.g., strawberries, blueberries, raspberries)
- 1/4 cup honey or maple syrup (adjust to taste)
- 1 tablespoon cornstarch or arrowroot powder
- 1 tablespoon lemon juice

Instructions:

1. **Preheat Oven:**
    - Preheat your oven to 350°F (175°C). Line an 8x8-inch baking dish with parchment paper, leaving an overhang for easy removal.
2. **Prepare Crust and Topping:**
    - In a large bowl, combine the rolled oats, almond flour, melted coconut oil (or butter), honey (or maple syrup), brown sugar (if using), salt, and ground cinnamon. Mix until well combined.
3. **Press and Bake Crust:**
    - Press about 2/3 of the oat mixture evenly into the bottom of the prepared baking dish to form the crust. Bake in the preheated oven for 10-12 minutes, or until the edges are lightly golden.
4. **Prepare Berry Filling:**
    - While the crust is baking, prepare the berry filling. In a medium saucepan, combine the mixed berries, honey (or maple syrup), cornstarch (or arrowroot powder), and lemon juice. Cook over medium heat, stirring occasionally, until the berries have broken down and the mixture has thickened (about 5-7 minutes). Remove from heat and let cool slightly.
5. **Assemble Bars:**
    - Once the crust is done baking, remove it from the oven and spread the berry filling evenly over the crust. Sprinkle the remaining oat mixture on top of the berries.
6. **Bake Bars:**

- Return the baking dish to the oven and bake for an additional 20-25 minutes, or until the topping is golden brown and the berry filling is bubbling.
7. **Cool and Slice:**
    - Allow the bars to cool completely in the baking dish on a wire rack before lifting out using the parchment paper overhang. Once cooled, cut into squares or bars.
8. **Store:**
    - Store the bars in an airtight container at room temperature for up to 3 days or in the refrigerator for up to 1 week.

These Oat and Berry Bars are perfect for a healthy snack or a quick breakfast and are packed with the goodness of oats and berries!

Pineapple Coconut Chia Pudding

Ingredients:

- 1 cup coconut milk (canned or carton, depending on your preference)
- 1/2 cup pineapple juice (freshly squeezed or from a carton)
- 1/4 cup chia seeds
- 2 tablespoons maple syrup or honey (adjust to taste)
- 1/2 teaspoon vanilla extract
- 1/2 cup fresh pineapple chunks (for topping)
- Shredded coconut (for garnish, optional)

Instructions:

1. **Combine Ingredients:**
   - In a medium bowl or jar, whisk together the coconut milk, pineapple juice, chia seeds, maple syrup (or honey), and vanilla extract.
2. **Mix Well:**
   - Stir well to ensure the chia seeds are evenly distributed and not clumped together.
3. **Chill:**
   - Cover the bowl or jar and refrigerate for at least 4 hours, or overnight. The chia seeds will absorb the liquid and turn into a pudding-like consistency.
4. **Stir Before Serving:**
   - After chilling, stir the pudding to make sure it's smooth and the chia seeds are well distributed.
5. **Serve:**
   - Spoon the chia pudding into serving bowls or glasses. Top with fresh pineapple chunks and a sprinkle of shredded coconut if desired.
6. **Garnish (Optional):**
   - For extra flavor and texture, you can also add a few fresh mint leaves or a drizzle of extra honey.

Storage:

- Store any leftover chia pudding in an airtight container in the refrigerator for up to 5 days.

This Pineapple Coconut Chia Pudding is a deliciously tropical treat that's perfect for breakfast or a light dessert!

Matcha Green Tea Ice Cream

Ingredients:

- 2 cups heavy cream
- 1 cup whole milk
- 3/4 cup granulated sugar
- 4 large egg yolks
- 2 tablespoons matcha green tea powder (culinary grade)
- 1 teaspoon vanilla extract
- A pinch of salt

Instructions:

1. **Heat Cream and Milk:**
   - In a medium saucepan, combine the heavy cream, whole milk, and granulated sugar. Heat over medium heat, stirring occasionally, until the mixture is hot and the sugar is dissolved, but not boiling.
2. **Prepare Egg Yolks:**
   - In a separate bowl, whisk the egg yolks until they are slightly thickened and pale in color.
3. **Temper the Egg Yolks:**
   - Gradually ladle a small amount of the hot cream mixture into the egg yolks, whisking constantly to temper them. This helps to gradually increase the temperature of the egg yolks without scrambling them.
4. **Combine and Cook:**
   - Pour the tempered egg yolk mixture back into the saucepan with the remaining cream mixture. Cook over medium heat, stirring constantly with a wooden spoon or silicone spatula, until the mixture thickens and coats the back of the spoon (about 170°F to 175°F or 77°C to 80°C).
5. **Dissolve Matcha:**
   - In a small bowl, whisk the matcha green tea powder with a few tablespoons of the hot cream mixture until smooth and free of lumps.
6. **Combine and Strain:**
   - Whisk the matcha mixture into the custard base until well combined. Remove the saucepan from heat. Pour the mixture through a fine-mesh strainer into a clean bowl to remove any potential lumps and ensure a smooth texture.
7. **Cool and Chill:**
   - Let the mixture cool to room temperature. Cover and refrigerate for at least 4 hours, or preferably overnight, to chill thoroughly.
8. **Churn Ice Cream:**
   - Once chilled, pour the mixture into an ice cream maker and churn according to the manufacturer's instructions, usually about 20-25 minutes.
9. **Freeze:**

- Transfer the churned ice cream to an airtight container and freeze for at least 2 hours to firm up.
10. **Serve:**
    - Scoop and enjoy the creamy matcha green tea ice cream.

Storage:

- Store leftover ice cream in an airtight container in the freezer for up to 2 weeks.

This Matcha Green Tea Ice Cream has a delightful, earthy flavor and a rich, creamy texture that's perfect for a refreshing treat. Enjoy!

Caramelized Banana Slices

Ingredients:

- 2 ripe bananas
- 2 tablespoons unsalted butter
- 2 tablespoons brown sugar
- 1/2 teaspoon ground cinnamon (optional)
- A pinch of salt
- Vanilla ice cream or Greek yogurt (optional, for serving)

Instructions:

1. **Prepare Bananas:**
    - Peel the bananas and slice them into 1/4-inch thick rounds.
2. **Melt Butter:**
    - In a large non-stick skillet, melt the butter over medium heat.
3. **Add Sugar and Cinnamon:**
    - Stir in the brown sugar and ground cinnamon (if using). Cook for about 1 minute, until the sugar starts to dissolve and form a syrup.
4. **Caramelize Bananas:**
    - Add the banana slices to the skillet in a single layer. Cook for about 2-3 minutes on each side, or until the bananas are golden brown and caramelized. Be careful not to overcook them, as they can become too soft and mushy.
5. **Add Salt:**
    - Once the bananas are caramelized, sprinkle a pinch of salt over them to enhance the flavors.
6. **Serve:**
    - Remove the caramelized bananas from the skillet and serve warm. They are delicious on their own or served over vanilla ice cream or Greek yogurt.

Optional Garnishes:

- Drizzle with extra caramel sauce or sprinkle with chopped nuts (like walnuts or pecans) for added texture and flavor.

Storage:

- Caramelized bananas are best enjoyed immediately. If you have leftovers, store them in an airtight container in the refrigerator for up to 1 day, but they may become softer upon reheating.

These Caramelized Banana Slices are a quick and indulgent treat that can be used as a topping for desserts, breakfasts, or just enjoyed by themselves!

Vegan Chocolate Avocado Pudding

Ingredients:

- 2 ripe avocados
- 1/4 cup unsweetened cocoa powder
- 1/4 cup maple syrup or agave syrup (adjust to taste)
- 1/4 cup coconut milk (or any non-dairy milk)
- 1 teaspoon vanilla extract
- A pinch of salt

Instructions:

1. **Prepare Avocados:**
   - Peel and pit the avocados. Scoop the flesh into a blender or food processor.
2. **Add Ingredients:**
   - Add the unsweetened cocoa powder, maple syrup (or agave syrup), coconut milk (or other non-dairy milk), vanilla extract, and a pinch of salt to the blender with the avocados.
3. **Blend:**
   - Blend on high speed until the mixture is smooth and creamy. You may need to stop and scrape down the sides of the blender or food processor to ensure everything is well combined.
4. **Adjust Sweetness:**
   - Taste the pudding and adjust the sweetness if needed by adding more maple syrup or agave syrup.
5. **Chill:**
   - Transfer the pudding to serving dishes or bowls and refrigerate for at least 1 hour to allow the flavors to meld and the pudding to firm up.
6. **Serve:**
   - Serve chilled. Optionally, garnish with fresh berries, a dollop of coconut whipped cream, or a sprinkle of shaved chocolate.

Storage:

- Store any leftover pudding in an airtight container in the refrigerator for up to 3 days. Stir well before serving, as it may thicken slightly upon chilling.

This Vegan Chocolate Avocado Pudding is a rich and creamy dessert that's not only dairy-free but also packed with healthy fats from the avocados. Enjoy!

Cinnamon Roasted Almonds

Ingredients:

- 2 cups raw almonds
- 1 tablespoon olive oil or melted coconut oil
- 2 tablespoons maple syrup or honey
- 1 tablespoon ground cinnamon
- 1/4 teaspoon salt
- 1/4 teaspoon ground nutmeg (optional, for extra flavor)
- 1/4 cup chopped pecans or walnuts (optional, for added crunch)

Instructions:

1. **Preheat Oven:**
   - Preheat your oven to 350°F (175°C). Line a baking sheet with parchment paper or a silicone baking mat.
2. **Prepare Almonds:**
   - In a large bowl, combine the almonds with the olive oil (or melted coconut oil), maple syrup (or honey), ground cinnamon, salt, and nutmeg (if using). Toss well to coat the almonds evenly.
3. **Spread Almonds:**
   - Spread the coated almonds in a single layer on the prepared baking sheet.
4. **Roast Almonds:**
   - Roast in the preheated oven for 10-15 minutes, stirring once halfway through the roasting time. Keep a close eye on them to prevent burning. The almonds should be golden brown and fragrant when done.
5. **Add Optional Nuts:**
   - If using, sprinkle the chopped pecans or walnuts over the almonds during the last 5 minutes of roasting for added texture and flavor.
6. **Cool:**
   - Remove the baking sheet from the oven and let the almonds cool completely on the baking sheet. They will crisp up further as they cool.
7. **Store:**
   - Store the cooled cinnamon roasted almonds in an airtight container at room temperature for up to 2 weeks.

These Cinnamon Roasted Almonds are a perfect snack for any time of the day and make a great addition to salads, yogurt, or as a topping for desserts!

Blueberry Yogurt Muffins

Ingredients:

- 1 1/2 cups all-purpose flour (or whole wheat flour for a healthier option)
- 1/2 cup granulated sugar (or coconut sugar)
- 1/2 teaspoon baking powder
- 1/2 teaspoon baking soda
- 1/4 teaspoon salt
- 1/2 teaspoon ground cinnamon (optional)
- 1/2 cup plain Greek yogurt (or regular yogurt)
- 1/4 cup milk (or a non-dairy milk of your choice)
- 1/4 cup melted coconut oil or unsalted butter
- 1 large egg
- 1 teaspoon vanilla extract
- 1 cup fresh or frozen blueberries (if using frozen, do not thaw)

Instructions:

1. **Preheat Oven:**
   - Preheat your oven to 375°F (190°C). Line a muffin tin with paper liners or lightly grease the muffin cups.
2. **Mix Dry Ingredients:**
   - In a large bowl, whisk together the flour, sugar, baking powder, baking soda, salt, and ground cinnamon (if using).
3. **Mix Wet Ingredients:**
   - In a separate bowl, combine the Greek yogurt, milk, melted coconut oil (or butter), egg, and vanilla extract. Mix until well combined.
4. **Combine:**
   - Pour the wet ingredients into the dry ingredients and gently fold until just combined. Be careful not to overmix, as this can result in dense muffins.
5. **Fold in Blueberries:**
   - Gently fold in the blueberries, being careful not to overwork the batter.
6. **Spoon into Muffin Tin:**
   - Divide the batter evenly among the muffin cups, filling each about 2/3 full.
7. **Bake:**
   - Bake in the preheated oven for 18-22 minutes, or until a toothpick inserted into the center of a muffin comes out clean and the tops are golden brown.
8. **Cool:**
   - Allow the muffins to cool in the tin for about 5 minutes before transferring them to a wire rack to cool completely.

Storage:

- Store the muffins in an airtight container at room temperature for up to 3 days, or freeze them for longer storage.

These Blueberry Yogurt Muffins are moist, tender, and bursting with juicy blueberries. They make a perfect breakfast or snack!

Fig and Walnut Energy Balls

Ingredients:

- 1 cup dried figs (stems removed)
- 1 cup walnuts (or any nuts of your choice)
- 1/4 cup rolled oats
- 1 tablespoon chia seeds or flax seeds (optional, for added nutrition)
- 1 tablespoon honey or maple syrup (optional, for added sweetness)
- 1/2 teaspoon vanilla extract
- A pinch of sea salt

Instructions:

1. **Prepare Ingredients:**
   - If the dried figs are not soft, soak them in warm water for about 10 minutes, then drain well.
2. **Process Nuts:**
   - In a food processor, pulse the walnuts until they are finely chopped but not ground into a powder. You want them to have some texture.
3. **Combine Ingredients:**
   - Add the dried figs, rolled oats, chia seeds (or flax seeds, if using), honey (or maple syrup), vanilla extract, and a pinch of sea salt to the food processor.
4. **Blend:**
   - Process the mixture until it starts to come together and forms a sticky dough. You may need to stop and scrape down the sides of the bowl occasionally.
5. **Form Balls:**
   - Scoop out small amounts of the mixture and roll them into bite-sized balls using your hands.
6. **Chill:**
   - Place the energy balls on a parchment-lined tray or plate. Refrigerate for at least 30 minutes to firm up.
7. **Store:**
   - Store the energy balls in an airtight container in the refrigerator for up to 2 weeks or freeze for longer storage.

Optional Coating:

- If you like, you can roll the energy balls in shredded coconut, cocoa powder, or crushed nuts for added flavor and texture.

These Fig and Walnut Energy Balls are perfect for a quick snack, a pre-workout boost, or a healthy treat on the go!

Low-Calorie Strawberry Shortcake

Ingredients:

For the Shortcakes:

- 1 cup whole wheat flour
- 1/4 cup granulated sugar or coconut sugar
- 1 1/2 teaspoons baking powder
- 1/4 teaspoon salt
- 1/4 cup cold unsalted butter or coconut oil
- 1/2 cup low-fat Greek yogurt
- 1/4 cup low-fat milk (or a non-dairy milk of your choice)
- 1 teaspoon vanilla extract

For the Strawberry Topping:

- 2 cups fresh strawberries, hulled and sliced
- 1 tablespoon honey or maple syrup
- 1 teaspoon lemon juice

For the Light Whipped Cream:

- 1 cup light whipped topping (store-bought or homemade with coconut cream or Greek yogurt)
- 1 teaspoon vanilla extract (if using Greek yogurt, sweeten to taste)

Instructions:

1. **Prepare Strawberries:**
    - In a medium bowl, toss the sliced strawberries with honey (or maple syrup) and lemon juice. Let sit for at least 30 minutes to allow the strawberries to release their juices.
2. **Preheat Oven:**
    - Preheat your oven to 375°F (190°C). Line a baking sheet with parchment paper.
3. **Make Shortcakes:**
    - In a large bowl, whisk together the whole wheat flour, granulated sugar, baking powder, and salt.
    - Cut the cold butter or coconut oil into the flour mixture using a pastry cutter or your fingers until the mixture resembles coarse crumbs.
    - Stir in the Greek yogurt, milk, and vanilla extract until just combined. The dough will be slightly sticky.
4. **Shape and Bake:**
    - Turn the dough onto a lightly floured surface and gently knead a few times. Pat the dough to about 1-inch thickness. Use a biscuit cutter or a glass to cut out rounds of dough.

- Place the shortcakes on the prepared baking sheet and bake for 12-15 minutes, or until the tops are golden brown. Allow to cool slightly.
5. **Prepare Whipped Cream:**
    - If using store-bought light whipped topping, just add vanilla extract if desired. If making homemade whipped cream with Greek yogurt, whip it until it's fluffy and sweeten to taste.
6. **Assemble Shortcakes:**
    - Slice the cooled shortcakes in half horizontally. Spoon some of the strawberries and their juices over the bottom half of each shortcake. Add a dollop of the light whipped cream, then place the top half of the shortcake on top.
7. **Serve:**
    - Serve immediately, garnished with extra strawberries or a sprig of mint if desired.

Storage:

- The shortcakes and strawberry topping can be stored separately in the refrigerator for up to 2 days. Assemble the shortcakes just before serving to keep them fresh.

This low-calorie Strawberry Shortcake offers a lighter take on the classic dessert without sacrificing flavor. Enjoy!

Poppy Seed Lemon Cake

Ingredients:

For the Cake:

- 1 1/2 cups all-purpose flour
- 1/2 cup granulated sugar
- 2 tablespoons poppy seeds
- 1 1/2 teaspoons baking powder
- 1/4 teaspoon baking soda
- 1/4 teaspoon salt
- 1/2 cup Greek yogurt (plain or vanilla)
- 1/4 cup unsweetened applesauce
- 1/4 cup vegetable oil or melted coconut oil
- 2 large eggs
- 1/4 cup freshly squeezed lemon juice
- 1 tablespoon lemon zest
- 1 teaspoon vanilla extract

For the Glaze (optional):

- 1/2 cup powdered sugar
- 1-2 tablespoons lemon juice

Instructions:

1. **Preheat Oven:**
   - Preheat your oven to 350°F (175°C). Grease and flour a 9-inch round cake pan or line it with parchment paper.
2. **Mix Dry Ingredients:**
   - In a medium bowl, whisk together the flour, granulated sugar, poppy seeds, baking powder, baking soda, and salt.
3. **Mix Wet Ingredients:**
   - In a large bowl, combine the Greek yogurt, applesauce, vegetable oil (or melted coconut oil), eggs, lemon juice, lemon zest, and vanilla extract. Whisk until smooth.
4. **Combine:**
   - Gradually add the dry ingredients to the wet ingredients, mixing gently until just combined. Be careful not to overmix.
5. **Bake:**
   - Pour the batter into the prepared cake pan and spread it evenly. Bake in the preheated oven for 25-30 minutes, or until a toothpick inserted into the center comes out clean and the cake is golden brown.
6. **Cool:**

    - Allow the cake to cool in the pan for 10 minutes, then transfer it to a wire rack to cool completely.
7. **Prepare Glaze (Optional):**
    - While the cake is cooling, make the glaze by whisking together the powdered sugar and lemon juice until smooth. Adjust the consistency by adding more lemon juice if needed.
8. **Glaze the Cake:**
    - Once the cake has cooled completely, drizzle the glaze over the top of the cake.
9. **Serve:**
    - Slice and serve the cake. It pairs beautifully with a cup of tea or coffee.

Storage:

- Store leftover cake in an airtight container at room temperature for up to 3 days, or in the refrigerator for up to 1 week.

This Poppy Seed Lemon Cake is light, moist, and packed with bright lemon flavor, making it a perfect treat for any occasion!

Dark Chocolate-Covered Banana Bites

Ingredients:

- 2 ripe bananas
- 1 cup dark chocolate chips (or chopped dark chocolate)
- 1 tablespoon coconut oil or butter (to help with melting)
- Optional toppings: sea salt, crushed nuts, shredded coconut

Instructions:

1. **Prepare Bananas:**
    - Peel the bananas and slice them into 1/2-inch thick rounds.
2. **Melt Chocolate:**
    - In a microwave-safe bowl, combine the dark chocolate chips and coconut oil (or butter). Microwave in 30-second intervals, stirring after each interval, until the chocolate is completely melted and smooth. Alternatively, you can melt the chocolate using a double boiler.
3. **Dip Banana Slices:**
    - Line a baking sheet with parchment paper. Using a fork or toothpick, dip each banana slice into the melted chocolate, coating it completely. Allow excess chocolate to drip off.
4. **Place on Baking Sheet:**
    - Place the coated banana slices on the parchment-lined baking sheet.
5. **Add Toppings (Optional):**
    - While the chocolate is still wet, sprinkle the banana bites with a small pinch of sea salt, crushed nuts, or shredded coconut, if desired.
6. **Chill:**
    - Place the baking sheet in the refrigerator or freezer for about 15-30 minutes, or until the chocolate is set and hardened.
7. **Serve:**
    - Once the chocolate has hardened, remove the banana bites from the parchment paper and serve.

Storage:

- Store any leftover banana bites in an airtight container in the refrigerator for up to 1 week, or in the freezer for up to 1 month.

These Dark Chocolate-Covered Banana Bites are a perfect combination of creamy bananas and rich chocolate, making them a delightful and healthy treat!

Orange and Almond Cake

Ingredients:

- **For the Cake:**
    - 2 large oranges
    - 1 1/2 cups almond meal (or finely ground almonds)
    - 1 cup granulated sugar or coconut sugar
    - 4 large eggs
    - 1 teaspoon baking powder
    - 1/4 teaspoon salt
    - 1/2 teaspoon vanilla extract
    - 1/4 cup melted coconut oil or unsalted butter (cooled)
- **For the Glaze (optional):**
    - 1/2 cup powdered sugar
    - 2-3 tablespoons freshly squeezed orange juice

Instructions:

1. **Prepare Oranges:**
    - Preheat your oven to 350°F (175°C). Grease and line a 9-inch round cake pan with parchment paper.
    - Wash the oranges and place them in a saucepan. Cover with water and bring to a boil. Reduce the heat and simmer for about 1 hour, until the oranges are tender. Drain and let them cool.
2. **Prepare the Cake:**
    - Once the oranges are cool, cut them into quarters and remove any seeds. Place the whole oranges (including the peel) in a food processor and blend until smooth.
    - In a large bowl, whisk together the almond meal, sugar, baking powder, and salt.
    - Add the orange puree, eggs, vanilla extract, and melted coconut oil (or butter) to the dry ingredients. Mix until just combined.
3. **Bake the Cake:**
    - Pour the batter into the prepared cake pan and spread it evenly.
    - Bake in the preheated oven for 30-35 minutes, or until a toothpick inserted into the center comes out clean and the cake is golden brown.
4. **Cool:**
    - Allow the cake to cool in the pan for 10 minutes, then transfer it to a wire rack to cool completely.
5. **Prepare Glaze (Optional):**
    - If using a glaze, whisk together the powdered sugar and orange juice until smooth. Adjust the consistency by adding more juice or sugar if needed.
6. **Glaze the Cake (Optional):**
    - Once the cake has cooled, drizzle the glaze over the top of the cake.
7. **Serve:**

    - Slice and serve. The cake is delicious on its own or with a light dusting of powdered sugar.

Storage:

- Store the cake in an airtight container at room temperature for up to 3 days, or in the refrigerator for up to 1 week.

This Orange and Almond Cake is wonderfully moist and flavorful, with a lovely citrusy twist that pairs perfectly with a cup of tea or coffee!

Spiced Pear Compote

Ingredients:

- 4 ripe pears (such as Bosc or Anjou), peeled, cored, and diced
- 1/4 cup granulated sugar or maple syrup (adjust to taste)
- 1/4 cup water
- 1 teaspoon ground cinnamon
- 1/4 teaspoon ground nutmeg
- 1/4 teaspoon ground ginger
- 1 tablespoon lemon juice
- 1 teaspoon vanilla extract (optional)

Instructions:

1. **Prepare Pears:**
    - Peel, core, and dice the pears into bite-sized pieces.
2. **Cook Pears:**
    - In a medium saucepan, combine the diced pears, sugar (or maple syrup), water, cinnamon, nutmeg, and ginger. Stir to combine.
3. **Simmer:**
    - Bring the mixture to a boil over medium heat. Reduce the heat and let it simmer, uncovered, for about 10-15 minutes, or until the pears are tender and the sauce has thickened slightly. Stir occasionally.
4. **Add Lemon Juice and Vanilla (Optional):**
    - Once the pears are tender, stir in the lemon juice and vanilla extract (if using). This will enhance the flavors and add a touch of brightness.
5. **Cool:**
    - Remove the compote from heat and let it cool slightly before serving. It will continue to thicken as it cools.
6. **Serve:**
    - Serve warm or at room temperature. The Spiced Pear Compote is delicious over yogurt, oatmeal, pancakes, waffles, or as a topping for desserts.

Storage:

- Store any leftover compote in an airtight container in the refrigerator for up to 1 week. It can also be frozen for up to 3 months.

This Spiced Pear Compote is wonderfully fragrant with warming spices and makes a cozy addition to many dishes!

Strawberry Coconut Chia Bars

Ingredients:

For the Bars:

- 1 cup rolled oats
- 1/2 cup shredded coconut (unsweetened)
- 1/2 cup almond meal or finely ground almonds
- 1/4 cup chia seeds
- 1/4 cup honey or maple syrup
- 1/4 cup coconut oil, melted
- 1/2 cup dried strawberries, chopped (or fresh strawberries, finely diced)
- 1/2 teaspoon vanilla extract
- A pinch of salt

For the Topping (optional):

- 2 tablespoons shredded coconut
- 2 tablespoons chopped dried strawberries

Instructions:

1. **Prepare Ingredients:**
    - Preheat your oven to 350°F (175°C). Line an 8x8-inch baking pan with parchment paper, leaving some overhang for easy removal.
2. **Mix Dry Ingredients:**
    - In a large bowl, combine the rolled oats, shredded coconut, almond meal, chia seeds, and a pinch of salt.
3. **Combine Wet Ingredients:**
    - In a separate bowl, whisk together the honey (or maple syrup), melted coconut oil, and vanilla extract.
4. **Combine Mixtures:**
    - Pour the wet ingredients over the dry ingredients and mix until well combined. Stir in the chopped dried strawberries (or diced fresh strawberries).
5. **Press into Pan:**
    - Transfer the mixture to the prepared baking pan and press it down firmly with the back of a spoon or your hands to ensure it is evenly packed.
6. **Add Topping (Optional):**
    - If using, sprinkle the top with shredded coconut and chopped dried strawberries.
7. **Bake:**
    - Bake in the preheated oven for 20-25 minutes, or until the edges are golden brown and the center is set.
8. **Cool and Cut:**

- Allow the bars to cool completely in the pan before lifting them out using the parchment paper. Cut into squares or bars.
9. **Store:**
    - Store the bars in an airtight container at room temperature for up to 1 week, or in the refrigerator for up to 2 weeks. They can also be frozen for longer storage.

These Strawberry Coconut Chia Bars are a great snack for on-the-go, packed with nutrients and bursting with sweet strawberry flavor. Enjoy!

Peach and Yogurt Smoothie

Ingredients:

- 1 cup fresh or frozen peaches (peeled and sliced)
- 1/2 cup plain Greek yogurt (or regular yogurt)
- 1/2 cup almond milk or any milk of your choice
- 1 tablespoon honey or maple syrup (adjust to taste)
- 1/2 teaspoon vanilla extract
- 1/2 cup ice cubes (optional, for a colder smoothie)
- Optional: 1 tablespoon chia seeds or flax seeds (for added nutrition)

Instructions:

1. **Prepare Ingredients:**
    - If using fresh peaches, peel and slice them. If using frozen peaches, there's no need to thaw them.
2. **Blend:**
    - In a blender, combine the peaches, Greek yogurt, almond milk, honey (or maple syrup), and vanilla extract.
3. **Add Ice (Optional):**
    - If you want a thicker, colder smoothie, add the ice cubes.
4. **Blend Until Smooth:**
    - Blend until the mixture is smooth and creamy. If needed, add a little more milk to reach your desired consistency.
5. **Add Seeds (Optional):**
    - If using chia seeds or flax seeds, add them to the blender and blend for an additional 10-15 seconds.
6. **Serve:**
    - Pour the smoothie into glasses and serve immediately.

Storage:

- Smoothies are best enjoyed fresh. If you need to store leftovers, keep them in an airtight container in the refrigerator for up to 24 hours. Stir or shake well before drinking, as ingredients may separate.

This Peach and Yogurt Smoothie is a tasty and nutritious way to start your day or enjoy as a mid-day snack!

Berry and Almond Crumble

Ingredients:

For the Filling:

- 3 cups mixed berries (such as strawberries, blueberries, raspberries, and blackberries)
- 1/4 cup granulated sugar or coconut sugar (adjust to taste)
- 1 tablespoon cornstarch or arrowroot powder
- 1 tablespoon lemon juice
- 1 teaspoon vanilla extract

For the Crumble Topping:

- 1 cup almond meal (or finely ground almonds)
- 1/2 cup rolled oats
- 1/4 cup chopped almonds (or any nuts of your choice)
- 1/4 cup coconut oil or unsalted butter, melted
- 1/4 cup granulated sugar or coconut sugar
- 1/2 teaspoon ground cinnamon
- A pinch of salt

Instructions:

1. **Prepare the Filling:**
    - Preheat your oven to 350°F (175°C).
    - In a large bowl, combine the mixed berries, sugar (or coconut sugar), cornstarch (or arrowroot powder), lemon juice, and vanilla extract. Toss to coat the berries evenly and set aside.
2. **Prepare the Crumble Topping:**
    - In a separate bowl, mix together the almond meal, rolled oats, chopped almonds, melted coconut oil (or butter), sugar (or coconut sugar), ground cinnamon, and a pinch of salt. Stir until the mixture is well combined and resembles coarse crumbs.
3. **Assemble the Crumble:**
    - Transfer the berry mixture to a baking dish (about 8x8 inches or similar size). Spread it out evenly.
    - Sprinkle the crumble topping evenly over the berry filling.
4. **Bake:**
    - Bake in the preheated oven for 30-35 minutes, or until the topping is golden brown and the berries are bubbling and tender.
5. **Cool:**
    - Allow the crumble to cool for a few minutes before serving. This will help the filling set slightly.
6. **Serve:**

- Serve warm, optionally with a dollop of Greek yogurt, vanilla ice cream, or a drizzle of cream.

Storage:

- Store leftovers in an airtight container in the refrigerator for up to 3 days. Reheat in the oven or microwave before serving. The crumble can also be frozen for up to 3 months; thaw and reheat before serving.

This Berry and Almond Crumble is a comforting and satisfying dessert that's perfect for any season and can be enjoyed with a variety of toppings!

Lemon Zest Energy Bites

Ingredients:

- 1 cup rolled oats
- 1/2 cup almond meal (or finely ground almonds)
- 1/4 cup chia seeds or flax seeds
- 1/4 cup honey or maple syrup
- 1/4 cup coconut oil or almond butter (melted if using coconut oil)
- Zest of 1 large lemon
- 2 tablespoons freshly squeezed lemon juice
- 1/2 teaspoon vanilla extract
- A pinch of salt

Instructions:

1. **Prepare Ingredients:**
   - In a large bowl, combine the rolled oats, almond meal, chia seeds (or flax seeds), and a pinch of salt.
2. **Mix Wet Ingredients:**
   - In a separate bowl, whisk together the honey (or maple syrup), melted coconut oil (or almond butter), lemon zest, lemon juice, and vanilla extract.
3. **Combine:**
   - Pour the wet ingredients into the dry ingredients. Stir until everything is well combined and the mixture starts to come together.
4. **Form Bites:**
   - Use your hands or a small cookie scoop to form the mixture into bite-sized balls (about 1 inch in diameter). Press firmly to ensure they hold their shape.
5. **Chill:**
   - Place the energy bites on a parchment-lined tray or plate. Refrigerate for at least 30 minutes to firm up.
6. **Store:**
   - Store the energy bites in an airtight container in the refrigerator for up to 1 week. They can also be frozen for up to 3 months. Just thaw before eating.

These Lemon Zest Energy Bites are bright, zesty, and packed with nutrients—perfect for a quick snack or a healthy treat!

Frozen Yogurt Bark with Fruit

Ingredients:

- 2 cups Greek yogurt (plain or vanilla)
- 2-3 tablespoons honey or maple syrup (adjust to taste)
- 1 teaspoon vanilla extract
- 1/2 cup fresh fruit (such as berries, diced kiwi, mango, or thinly sliced strawberries)
- Optional: 2 tablespoons granola or nuts (chopped), for topping

Instructions:

1. **Prepare Yogurt Mixture:**
   - In a medium bowl, mix the Greek yogurt, honey (or maple syrup), and vanilla extract until smooth and well combined.
2. **Prepare Baking Sheet:**
   - Line a baking sheet with parchment paper or a silicone baking mat.
3. **Spread Yogurt:**
   - Pour the yogurt mixture onto the prepared baking sheet. Use a spatula to spread it into an even layer, about 1/4 to 1/2 inch thick.
4. **Add Fruit and Toppings:**
   - Evenly distribute your chosen fruit over the yogurt layer. If using, sprinkle granola or chopped nuts on top.
5. **Freeze:**
   - Place the baking sheet in the freezer and freeze for at least 2 hours, or until the yogurt is completely frozen and firm.
6. **Break into Pieces:**
   - Once frozen, remove the bark from the freezer and break it into pieces or shards.
7. **Serve and Store:**
   - Serve immediately, or store the pieces in an airtight container in the freezer for up to 2 weeks.

Tips:

- For a different flavor, you can mix in a bit of cocoa powder or fruit puree into the yogurt before spreading it on the baking sheet.
- You can also use dried fruit or a drizzle of nut butter if fresh fruit is not available.

This Frozen Yogurt Bark with Fruit is a fun, customizable, and healthy dessert or snack that's sure to please!

www.ingramcontent.com/pod-product-compliance
Lightning Source LLC
LaVergne TN
LVHW061949070526
838199LV00060B/4037